Putting on
my species

Sasja Janssen

Putting on my species

translated from the Dutch by
Michele Hutchison

Shearsman Books

First published in the United Kingdom in 2020 by
Shearsman Books Ltd
PO Box 4239
Swindon
SN3 9FN

Shearsman Books Ltd Registered Office
30–31 St. James Place, Mangotsfield, Bristol BS16 9JB
(this address not for correspondence)

www.shearsman.com

ISBN 978-1-84861-705-6

Originally published in Dutch as *Ik trek mijn species aan*
copyright © Sasja Janssen,
by Em Querido's Uitgeverij, Amsterdam, 2014

Introduction and translations copyright © Michele Hutchison, 2020

This book was published with the support of
the Dutch Foundation for Literature.

N ederlands
N letterenfonds
dutch foundation
for literature

Contents

'that I am always and in everything helpless, powerless and as replaceable as an atom'
          Willem Frederik Hermans, *Beyond Sleep*

ENOUGH POEMS ABOUT ME

Today I went crazy.
You should see it some time.
You should see it.
Comes from all this poetry maybe.
Yes, this poetry, everything is staged.
Enough poems about me.
Yes, enough, done with the staging.
They're also the full words, the actual days.
The real ones, you should feel them, what use they are.
It's because of the city, my love.
Were you intimate.
Were you secretive.
Everything was there.
And the landscape, it groped so fingerishly in your cavities.
They were twigs that grew inside my head.
Did you live behind the hours.
Yes, I knew the causes without their consequences.
Did you think about madness, did you love him.
I was so very fond of him.
I couldn't do without.
I wept when I laughed, I laughed when I wept.
You like to see that.
Yes, you should know.
You know.
But it's almost over.
Yes, delusion always finds a new love, so greedily
he adores.
But come, first take a look.

AND YET IT BEGINS

1

There was someone someone was
spread into the black sun like starlings made of dust
where she
in the tingling, buckling, in balloons that gracefully touched
a person was born of her own poison
and her holes burned the seething.

She cased darkness that fell into itself, fell
and at the same time existed, glare, profusion, hysteria around the edges
also those things without blood, the people their thoughts hornlike
until they broke meaning and played dead
in their bodies to make her beginning a beginning.

2

At first they were made of burning stars.

Someone made gender of them and like the world they mated manically.
And sex was made
she was her mouth her anus which she came out of, as opening as wound
that he had made bounce with that unusually hard thing his tipsy member
and his navel with her fingers.
It made you think of them even before the flesh was aware.

Then they had shed their hot skins.

3

The jawfish they loved more deeply
because they gave skeletons
and in the jaws behind the gills where biblical butterflies
began language that burst wherever it could
gushed out of their holes, moral oral, who says they don't pray to themselves
we like to talk our bones together.

4

Her tribes, the founders and their wild ones, the children
animals and the fruit, burst and green the skies
the trees with voices of sonar
ants with lines, writing.

Her beings: the touchable and the happy, the cunning and those with
        landsickness
the entertained, the made, the maimed and their creations
the rulers that wove their veins metallically, the odd one
in death's grip. Coming ready or not.

5

In the penultimate stage someone waited waited
and saw the people stiff heavens, simian nights made of pheromones
hell slung loosely around the neck
flecks fell from birds, quarks became heavy so heavy
milk dripped from the fields, girls danced in breasts, dancing
dervishly at once, to name one thing, someone had stopped giving names.

She treated herself to light in the throbbing crazily
and the people vomited people, they vomited her and once again
and even less than once the earth spoiled without her beauty.

6

She spun, she tumbled bowl-shaped, she wrung out milky ways.
Someone fell into great heights.

PUTTING ON MY SPECIES

1.

I was born from a dot at nine one morning
the first morning possible because it didn't come
out of night, it coloured from a bright fuchsia to a sulphurous yellow
I still remember that.

The right one, the right sharpness and size, made by someone
handed a 9H, briefly transfixed
they called her God apart from me.

A horrible first, but I finally stopped being
no one.

2.

I wore a swaddling cloth that would become a shroud
it's impossible, yet it is so.
Not far from here I became a dot again, the only one

but a weaker one, perhaps made by a 9B by that same
person, she corked me back into myself, the cottons continuing to
give off scent in my wardrobe.

3.

I believed things happened simultaneously.
Could be the species I had to put on, could be the movement
could be the happiness or craziness or both, rain with sunshine.

I believed it had to snow, thought behind it
and I grew into my own test card
deceptively identical, like any other's.

4.

I mastered living immediately and predicted what would happen next.
When love came not even in the guise
of a young angel I forgot my dot and caught fire, yellow
a fuchsia heart.

Then I forgot about forgetting, naked as a single rose.

5.

After that I took off my species, to see if I was empty
to see if I dared to, drained of blood I dared.

The others stared at the way I was, that there was nothing
left of me, should there be a remnant of me or something?

6.

I was instantly less good at living, you shouldn't take off what you can hardly get on, back into the cast became shapeless.

I AM MY SEX

Until today only words used, but had to
stop that, the windows steam up with our yeast

through the floundering, the falling, the tender, the nauseous
the sweet, the fleshy, the blueish dangling around each other's necks.

We sang ourselves. We had ourselves for the first time.

Only I have a cunt
like seaweed in a bath or skin stretched around a man
cold tiles, more often, that meat
there's that tight one, that sweet one but not pushing towards
a hard strip-lit afternoon if I am there and you are not.

I am my sex
away with those calf's legs meant to seduce
no belly that will heave, my breasts
if yes my breasts do something else
then my mind will settle on being something of quite a different category.

She leaves behind an ice-white man's shirt on a nail
a sweater that threatens my navel dirty grey, shoes for
an instep bared, the whitewashed wall alms for later when alone.

Comes says goodbye, look, bye-bye nirvana, why then
let yourself be covered one last time like a table without guests, a lickspittle
to go on the linen?

She spreads to the small smaller most charming most innermost part
where I see how abandoned I am.

The world is waiting for me beneath an elm
where I reflect upon snow and upon despising
reflecting upon snow due to a lyrical shortfall
in the summer.

Perhaps some drops of sake wait for me on his hand
that smells of milk and salt but the sky's
too wide for my blossoming tongue
my pussy.

THE STITCHES

The summer was broken and I took my sins
to the sewing shop, I couldn't decide between
button thread or basting thread, the tailor didn't help me, I was guilty
how could he forgive a thing like that.

The tailor unpacked my sins, they squirmed
in the bare light until I started feeling sorry for them
just like the ferns that topped themselves
just like you in the forest of Aokigahara.

Yellow snow fell and infidelity could not be threaded
but turned to felt with hot water, soap, vinegar, his felt needle
in my love juice, this man short, his memory blunt
praised split stitch, festoon stitch, leaf stitch
for what was threadbare, the seams bedevilled.

Behind his bead curtain I undressed myself
before my sins could take hold of me again
and there where
my dress tumbled around me in a circle
of ill-treated cotton
he stabbed with great fervour through my flesh
the seams of my sex
tangled like wool washed too hot.

The tailor shredded the last pretexts
from my skin and measured me up once
more inside, it was his triumph
I was ready-to-wear
threaded, sewn up, needled
my skirt uncombed, all my sins but two repaired
a lie on a ribbon and a forgotten penance.
I pawned them for some extra queen stitches
for the trip to the woods, I was perishable.

At the woods' edge I found the koan how to clap
with one hand and when I heard the sound, I knew it
I knew it cold
that the trees bore it
in the sky of bullets: you are here.

Longing was nothing in the air chambers
without my sins, where he led me to dance
one two out of this basin of bones comes no one.
We swam in jade, we laughed branches free
and chewed dentate cherry tree leaves.
The stems of my dress snapped, cochlear structure of branch and leaf
why did we need to hang?

Later a maple tree strangled a young salesman
his eyes on his cheeks, his pelvis split.
We rejoiced at the nuts in his suit
they tasted of fire.

I took a jackdaw from my belly blue-black
it left a smudge on my palm
it pecked more darkness into my skin.
It was as though we suddenly stopped hurrying
and forgot what we had to do among all those trunks
and logs, the jackdaw crept
back into me and sang my organs together.
We decided to continue for a while.

Come, you said
I'll show you the afternoons where we can live
the high afternoon hours, where the sky pulls
the veins from leaves, the trees suck our blood.
We plucked brightness from the sky, scraped vegetation
and ate our lips black.

As our bellies, our hands, our livers
our stomachs, our hearts, the garland of my hair, your fingers
those hours without catching pigment.
As you stabbed my heart

(double tack stitch, cross-stitch, flannel stitch
French and colonial knot stitch, blind seam stitch
perhaps the Holbein stitch, triple straight stitch
or the closed overlock, Armenian stitch, backstitch
tension stitch, pit stitch, not the horizontal mattress stitch
absolutely not that one)

after the last stitch we slept for days and nights
we couldn't be found.

Then you were king, I was queen.

SINCE I MUST TRAVEL

When the neighbour's dog gets sick and he wants to die
in a country where its barking sounds southerly
I travel to foreign parts with constant dog days
and I take with me a silver pill box
with the dose for death.
Are my feet light enough, my cheeks loose?
Il faut cultiver, the dog says.

I bear my boundlessness as a weapon
my blood against fevers and dengue fear
countless maps so that I know where not to go
my child jesus on a cross to show him
how he hangs in a country where the barking doesn't stop
until the morning. We have the same name, worship
the same ground, the dog and me.

In death in death
I undertook a journey, I took a lot with me
it took me ages to pack, but that night
that wasn't shaped like a blanket or carbon cloud
the way you think, I know how you think
misty, chemical, accentuated, loveish.

In death there was a sound
like paper that no longer has a use
or the whining of a hungry straw dog
a child that can't whistle very well
that kind of thing you thought, I know but
it's none of those three.

I am the only one
I'm lonelier than you
now I'm undertaking a large and expanding journey
in the armpit of my own death.

This area comes shyly
as shyly as a boy who doesn't know what to do with his blushing
sex in this landscape with the gleaming
white that hovers over it.

Sometimes a social animal appears, a lake
a rock, stacked-up cities, squares in the distance with people
hilly light over the pubic mounds around it all.
But everything is very still, as though under water.

I say very little in these parts too.
I can bet on whether I'll stay behind here. I can bet what will
leave me here. I bet like a boy who brings us off
on the purling moss.

Are these my holiday photos? I wear no shy
boy's seed, have seen no white skies
until someone says the images return, first hesitantly
but soon blazing like a heaven in flames, we see that often.

I CAN'T TAKE IT,
THAT FUSS ABOUT LIFE AND DEATH

1

Better skies on their way I promise. My diorama
has already birthed its youngest, stripped the heavens, trees
rivers, plants, not here yet.

My children fool open their clown's mouths, women
light fires and poke light that surges onto their shoulders
like tulle like tulle.

The surging is not simple, the light is, it allows itself to be caught.
I am so turned on.

And still wind comes, a beginner's error. Small tornados grow
from tulle, on heat but fierce when you know what's going to come.
Do I know what's going to come?

2

With antlers and bouncing tails the men shoot the vortexes
out of the sky, fuming at the extremities and full of toads and plague
a black I haven't seen before.

How can it be that I let them go already, I can't get my head around it.
The land wants to keep its thin furrows the way I bought it, no plague
but a world of only sand and clay, you don't set anyone down in that.

How tenderly he carries me, does he know why I'm kicking him out of
       the seams?

3

Dawn breaks with fluorine, spoiling all paleness.
Everything childishly simple, but my courage is firewood
in an organism that fishes for breath.

Back those bellies of the clouds and rains clattering everywhere.
The periodic table under the flat-bottomed boat, two rivers with arms
And feet, stones and fish, hills for depth, depths for ends.

And what else, say it. More people, bird, tree. I grab some things from
          brochures
I keep fear back in my bags, there has been no dying here
yet, here how softly those antlers walk.

Then the nights with a halo, fire circles things
fertile and prepares them for the great repetition.
Never before such a hurry, was there a before?

4

Even after the storms of the beginning the autumn rains come
they flatter and leave dew stones behind like on the lady's mantle
I forgot to plant. Everything disappoints me?

I buckle a belt tightly, my breath becomes snow. The men
are given furs around their waists, like in *Les saisons* by Maurice Pons.
The little clowns crawl in ice, their navels open, I recoil my zest for work.

Suddenly I wail an unearthly light into a dark boy
invent suicide, its body a broken horse on the riverbed.
See that I can't take it, that fuss about life and death.

5

I make my wife according to my own lustiness, but I
cannot take her along, she'd shrivel up. She shapes herself
supplely from my hand. Coos that this isn't her first time.

Why I am jealous and squeeze her my venom.
Her slender legs dangle outside the green-black diorama.
We couple two sons, not in my own image, I'm wary of

putting my own inheritance into them, how can I leave them otherwise?
My sons lip her all over and for the first time I'm glad of my strong hands.
Soon my sons are making sons from girls made of river clay

still in the plastic. I hang up constellations, wipe butterfly clouds
like eyes above the land, spread the birds and insects
bees bees inside.

6

His magnifying glass directed at me, dark as a cosmos. There the first
newest person is born in this sweltering greenhouse.
My wife fans her skirts and doesn't know who I am.

I bulge out of all my openings but tightly swaddled
I disappear, until spring's shoots and hormones wake
me up. Do I smell wild flowers, the ones I made?

Smell salty genitals, smell the newest people
sharp and challenging. The diorama turns away from me, the fish
teem their colours but words pale as I pick them up.

My wife knows they are viable but me?
They came out of me! They are me! I whisper.
Am I whispering?

7

A flaccid organ quivers up between the newest people
I pull on it, but they gesture with antlers for me to
leave, their language that is no language and sounds like wood on wood.

Once again I take sorrow about my sons and their sons
with the same sons and my hands die, where is my euphoria?
A firm slap launches me into my own world, small like all the rest.

I am the misprint in my work and blood shy for my own blood
I wait until they come, I see the fire, I hear them, a clapping noise
that swells, it turns me on, oh it turns me on, it is back
I am so turned on.

WAYS OF

Ways of walking

When the litmus paper is dipped
in stardust and always runs to violet and hopefully
humble blue, but it only becomes important when
green, yellow, orange or even red for predicting
a fruitful life ahead
then the days and nights have germinated.

If you get lost from top to somewhere bottom
you can't take as your mother used to tell you
the same coloured route back, it dries up
and pulverizes, but something light rises up
in a colour that doesn't appear on your litmus
a glimpse of another life long after you have
stopped, the days and nights recycled.

Ways of casting the dice

We have been cast together and his dark hands
are unknown to me, the small bones like twigs
smelling subcutaneously of tobacco and expensive powder
how many children how many women live in the palm of that hand
your death too.
His long nails, they chase me fear for later
when we
but first get out of that neck, that tight-fitting Sehnsucht.
What do eyes do when they play against each other?

It is the die
that crows sardonically again again
until I put on my neck, to trust my eyes.
The darkened man turns on the pissy light and asks if I like prawns.
I don't eat creatures that feature in fairytales
like you, he says and his eyes shoot
his sockets over me like marbles.

Ways of playing

I play chess with his hands because they are larger and not mine.
I play chess with his hands so that I escape the pleated time
that squeezes all.
I play chess with his hands because he is in a hurry to get away
from the start and I get ready, prefer not to stay in the middle.
I don't feel compelled to win or lose. Oh no? You are a fatal kind
of game, you want to get ahead of everything, even the game.

Ways of not having a hand in it

In the park a game has lost its player
who has spotted me, but I don't look up from my book
that keeps starting all over again without me having a hand in it
as though I have a hand in it, it is red from the cold, ragged cuticles.

A travelling salesman (stationery) that I forget
turns up again, a chalky pale girl with silent bosom
from a Russian story wants to be adored by him
but the travelling salesman falls back into his pages
in my hands, where he plays black against a corpulent man
who pants that a draw is like unconsummated love.

The game jumps onto my lap, a game too smells like a dog
fear of the real game, even one like the arch
moth-dog the game reminds me reluctantly of
and that sticks to my belly as no other lover.
Is that me here, with disconnected hands?

Ways of knowing

How hands know what they need to do: begin the right
beginning and not at the end of the previous game and right
before this new first move in which you reject me as a gambit.
I hesitate about my opening moves but my fingers
they stiffen when I think about you irrationally
I stay in check and glide into a trench bouncing

Deep as the Vitjaz's trough where prawns rake up
old sand and throw it up to no avail.
Returned too often from a love that was just beginning.

Ways of burying a hand

The milk boils over the enamel pan morning yellow
its base like fresh black earth, that fear
is not made of night howlers or of black bile or of the finite
the malicious bank and its poppies.
What is it made of then, small milk?

From deep gardens where aerial roots take away your breath
woodlice hide in your slit, fingers turn out of your
belly. I shrug my shoulders, stir the fire.
The handle against my midriff I feel small milk
mocking my hand hot, with fresh earth to bury it in.

FABULATE ME

I remember that life never wraps up
I remember the trips through the pale blue wide snow
I remember the dead pigs along the roadside
sleeping sweetly, they were still talking
I remember my first love who left me
I remember my mother, sometimes she is happy
I remember falling off my bike like a paper cut-out
on a viaduct in the frost
I remember my husband with shoulder blades like wings
I remember a procession in the spring village with ribbons
on the trees, dresses false white in the cutting sun
remember me
I remember my unborn child
I remember the city, its suburbs, the building girls threw themselves off
where I did my studies
I remember my rape in a central-heating-hot flat in Rome
I remember the architecture student, he survived without me
but I stayed with him
I remember my loves that surround me like a small planet
I remember the azure-blue café where I wasn't allowed to serve
a writer more than ten espressos, but he stopped counting himself
I remember the high-pitched singing with a girl in the meadows
she had sullen hair just like me, we knew what our beginning was
please go on
I remember the crackling night in which we made a son
I remember that dark mornings got stuck with transverse stars
I remember my longing like a vine
I remember my father, he had to die but had last words
I remember that my husband and I courted the sea
I remember the islands that we dug out like dogs
I remember my long hair that wore thin through sessions in rooms
chairs trams trains beds hands
remember me anyway

I remember the expensive bottles of wine my husband bought for me, for
him the ham with a foot, it made a soldier without regrets of me
I remember the arrival of my books, they weren't births
they'd always been there
I remember my son, his hands his blunt nails, why I cry
I remember my night fears, nights in a row, not nocturnal blue
but hellish orange
I remember my mother, they got married in secret
I remember my twin sister, we pushed our tongues together
I remember the poet because he taught me how to hear the dunes, we
were fond of each other but drove each other crazy
I remember the light, fish-silver lead thin grey ethereal green
do it then
I remember the division of body, not of body and soul
I remember the Dutch teacher, I was a doll in his bed
not his spring in Fialta
I remember the filmmaker who embraced me on paper and in real life
as no other because he embraced me on paper as only
a filmmaker can
I remember the Stendhal perfume I couldn't afford that fell onto the
bathroom floor which I went to lie in naked
I remember the houses I lived in, they took something from me
and don't want me back
I remember the consolation of Paustovsky who talks to me when he lies next
to me but I cannot console him because he is dust
I remember my poems, no one understands them
I remember fabulous, fabular me

ENOUGH POEMS ABOUT ME

You wanted to see it, what I had become.
Was it because of the children, they screamed
your dreams on sticks.
It was them, but I let them play.
Are you oversensitive.
From now on only the universe, steppes and seas, without an I.
Will I forget you?
Can I grab hold of you just one time everywhere.
Catch me if you can.
But I'm not it anymore, I'm already covered in mud.
I'm made of metallic rivers, the red earth.
Is it about the others?
I am the others.
It's the lust.
It's the longing.
I won't forget you.
Shhh, talking feeds madness.
I loved him so much.
I could no longer do without.
See how the world moves faster around us?
No, I can feel a green-gold beetle
in my chest, it walks me towards confusion.
Did he drive you wild, my love.
Do you want to ham it up one more time.
No, I've had enough.
I take it off, my species.
It is yours, do what you want with it.
Say bye. I say bye.

www.ingramcontent.com/pod-product-compliance
Lightning Source LLC
Chambersburg PA
CBHW031934080426
42734CB00007B/687